Helping Children See Jesus

ISBN: 978-1-64104-099-0

Praying Hyde
Missionary to India

Authors: Rose-Mae Carvin
Cover Illustrator: Linda McInturff
Computer Graphic Artists: Scott Gladfelter, Yuko Willoughby
Typesetting and Layout: Patricia Pope

© 2019 Bible Visuals International
PO Box 153, Akron, PA 17501-0153
Phone: (717) 859-1131
www.biblevisuals.org

All rights reserved. No part of this publication may be reproduced, stored in a retrieval system or transmitted in any form by any means, electronic, mechanical, photocopy, recording or otherwise, without the prior permission of the publisher, except as provided by USA copyright law. Published by Scripture Union in England and used by arrangement with them

RELATED ITEMS

For other formats of this story and related items, please visit www.biblevisuals.org and search using the title or the item #5480.

FREE TEXT DOWNAD

To access a FREE printable copy of the teaching text (PDF format) in English or other available languages, enter S5480DL in the search box. Add the item to your cart, and use coupon code XTACSV17 at checkout. Once your order is processed you will receive an email with a link to the free download.

STUDENT ACTIVITES

These are included with the FREE printable copy of the English teaching text for this story. See the directions under Free Text Download (above) to access them.

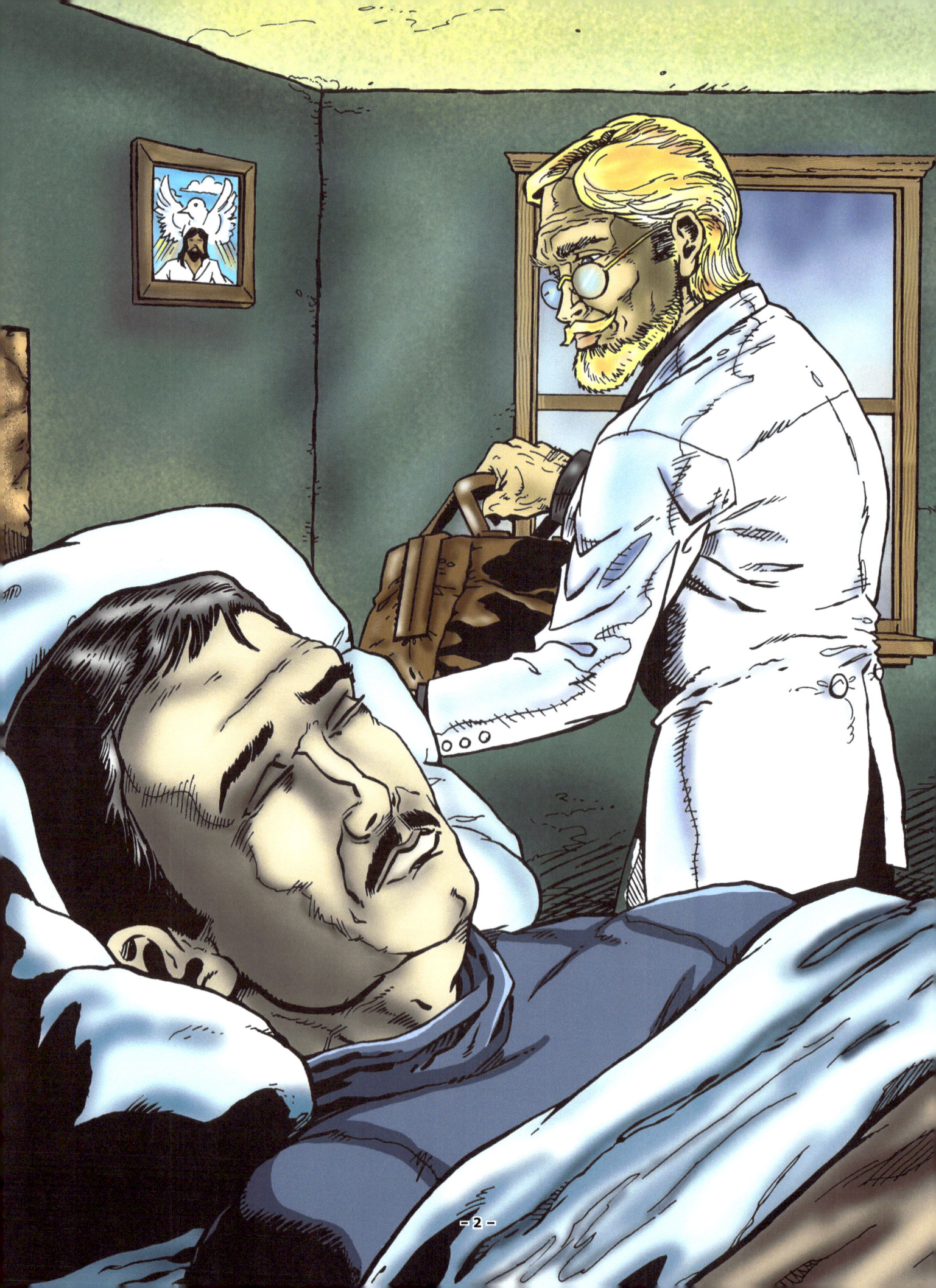

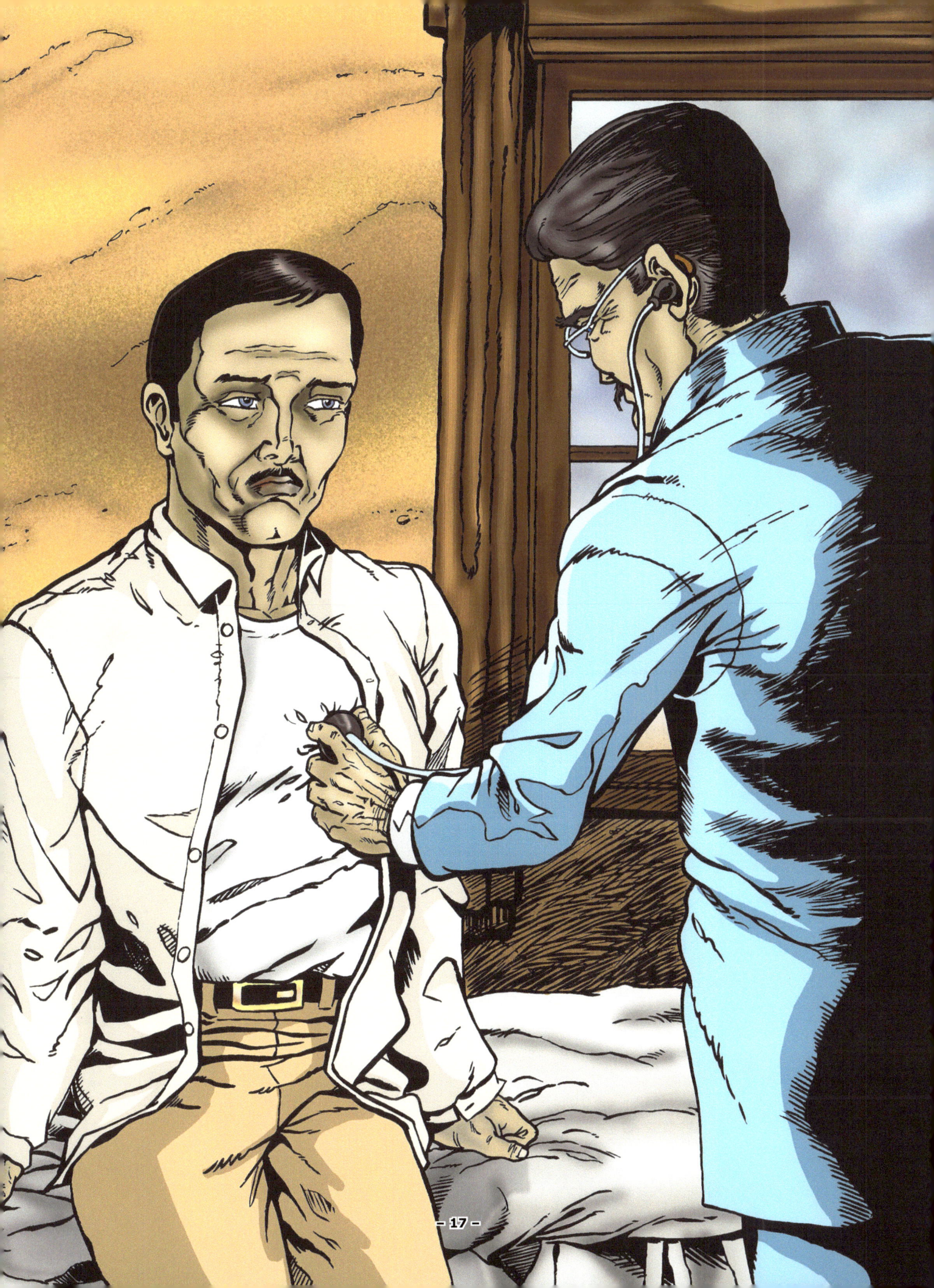

Pray, Pray, Pray;
the Bible says to pray
That reapers brave
may harvest save, lest
souls should die today!

That boys and girls who never heard

Be plainly told the blessed Word.

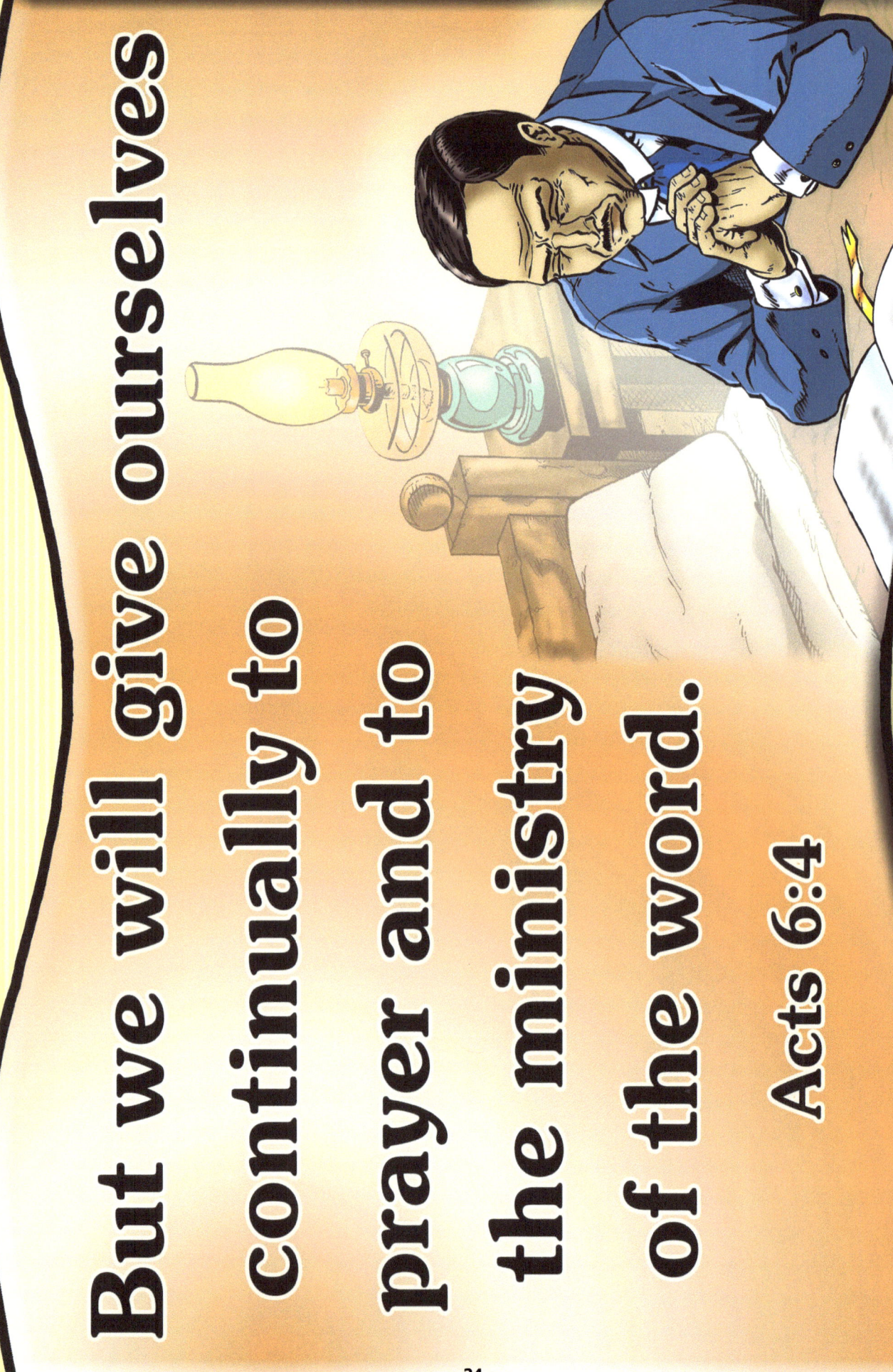

Chapter 1

INTRODUCTION

Do you have a nickname?

If you have, it probably tells something about you. An elderly woman had the nickname TIGER Bennett when she was a little girl. But she was not like a tiger when she grew up. She was dear and sweet and everyone loved her. She told thousands of children about the Lord Jesus who died for them.

Surely when the Lord said, "Frances, I want you to come home to Heaven now," there were many boys and girls already there to welcome her. More will follow her there because she led them to receive the Lord Jesus Who is the only way to Heaven.

No, as a woman, Frances Bennett was not like a tiger. Yet because that was her nickname when she was little, we know she must have been a fighter. Her nickname tells us this.

We are going to learn about John Hyde–a man who had a wonderful nickname: Praying Hyde. Would you like that for a nickname? Can you guess what kind of man he was to have earned such a nickname?

Did John Hyde offer beautiful prayers in public places where many people heard him? Did they talk about his beautiful prayers and so call him Praying Hyde? These questions will be answered in our story. Listen carefully!

Show Illustration #1

John Hyde was born in Illinois in 1865. His father, a minister, was good and kind to everyone. John's mother, a lovely Christian woman, was said to be "Christ like." John Hyde knew what it was to hear his mother and father pray. He learned to pray when he was small.

John had two brothers and three sisters. John's father often prayed, "Dear God, please send missionaries to far-off places [distant lands] where the people do not know about the Lord Jesus." So John's father was not surprised when two of his sons wanted to become missionaries.

One of John's older brothers was named Edmund. When he grew up, Edmund went away to school where he studied to be a missionary.

One summer Edmund was on vacation from school. Instead of going home, he went to the state of Montana. There he worked hard to get Sunday schools started.

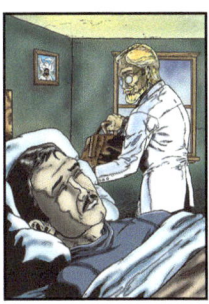

Show Illustration #2

One day Edmund became ill. The doctor said, "You have mountain fever. You must get home as quickly as you can."

So John's brother Edmund started for home. At that time the quickest way to travel was by train. And even that was not fast! To get from Montana to Illinois would take at least two days.

Friends knew that Edmund's fever might get so high that he would become delirious. So they pinned his railroad ticket to his coat. They wrote notes to the conductors who would be on the trains. The notes told where he was going and exactly what trains he had to take.

What a hard trip that must have been for a sick man to take alone! Back home, John and the rest of the family were praying for Edmund, though they did not know he was ill.

Edmund finally arrived home safely. How glad his family was to see him!

Show Illustration #3

How sad they were only a few days later when Edmund died. They didn't understand God's way. But they all knew how to pray, and so they did. God gave them peace in their hearts, even in their trouble.

Has He ever done this for you, too?

John had been planning to be a preacher in the United States. But after Edmund died, John felt the Lord wanted him to take his brother's place. At first John was not quite willing.

Show Illustration #4

It was during his last year in seminary (a school which trains ministers) that John stayed awake one night, all night long, praying. The next day his face was bright and shining. "It is settled," he told a classmate. John Hyde knew that God wanted him to go to some foreign land to preach the Gospel.

One of the nicest things about praying alone in our Quiet Time, is that we can be still and listen to God speak to us. We talk to Him, pray for others, and then we are quiet. God speaks in a still, small voice. We cannot hear Him with our human ears. But in our hearts we understand what He is saying to us.

Sometimes God causes us to remember some Scripture verses we have learned. We know His will through that verse. We must say, as the boy Samuel did so many years ago, "Speak, for Your servant hears."

John Hyde learned to talk to God for long hours. He learned to listen to God's voice. In time, God told John to which country he should go.

Chapter 2

Show Illustration #5

There was nothing to see but water and sky as the ship carried John Hyde across the ocean. Day after day for many weeks, John Hyde traveled. The waves were often high. Sometimes there were storms. But John Hyde prayed, and God protected the ship. Finally John stepped ashore in the land of India. For John Hyde had heard God's voice telling him he was to go to India to preach the Gospel. It was a difficult place for him to begin his missionary work. At first he did not do well.

Show Illustration #6

Though John studied diligently, he had a hard time learning the language. (This was probably partly due to his having defective hearing.) He felt he was a failure and became discouraged–so discouraged that he thought he should return home. But he never neglected his Bible study and prayer. God helped him to know he was to stay in India. So John worked on the language, praying earnestly for the Lord to help him.

Right from the beginning people realized that John Hyde knew how to talk to God. And they discovered that God answered John's prayers. Before long they called him Praying Hyde.

The people learned that Praying Hyde often stayed awake all night talking to God and listening to His voice. They did not hear him pray long prayers in public.

Praying Hyde did not pray only at night. Often during the day he talked with God in a little room. Many times he didn't take time to eat. "I'm not hungry," he would say and kept on praying.

God answered John's prayer about learning the difficult language. Soon the people of India said, "He speaks our language correctly and easily." Better than that, they exclaimed, "He speaks the language of Heaven, also!"

Praying Hyde did not pray for himself alone. It was for the souls of the people of India for whom he prayed most.

Show Illustration #7

He had seen the people bathing in the River Ganges hoping to wash away their sins. He had seen their funeral pyres (on which they burned the bodies of the dead). He had seen their idols and their temples. And he knew that though the people of India did the best they knew, they were lost because they had never received the Lord Jesus as Saviour. He could not bear the thought of their being separated eternally from God.

God heard John's prayers. Many began to listen gladly when he preached. Numbers placed their trust in the Saviour–the Lord Jesus. This made John Hyde happy. Yet he longed to see more coming to Christ. So he kept on praying long hours, all alone.

God spoke each day to John. He wants to speak to us as He did to Praying Hyde. Perhaps God has some special work for you to do. Maybe He cannot tell you about it because you do not get quiet before Him.

Remember: Praying Hyde lived and died many years ago. God could use many more praying people today in this world of ours. Perhaps He will use you, even now, while you are young. And perhaps God wants to tell you now His plan for your life.

Show Illustration #8

It was not easy for the people of India to leave the only religion they had ever known. Theirs was a religion of torturing themselves; of praying as often as five times a day–praying to an idol which had ears but could not hear; a religion of begging for a living.

To turn from idols to the true and living God, and to His Son, the Lord Jesus Christ, was not easy for the people in India. They needed to hear God's Word from those who belonged to Him. They needed the prayers of John Hyde. They need *your* prayers. Oh, who will pray? Oh, will *you* pray?

> **NOTE TO THE TEACHER**
>
> The words of the second stanza of the hymn "Be A Missionary" appear on page 20-22. It would be well to introduce that stanza here and sing it along with each succeeding chapter. Please explain the meaning of the unfamiliar expressions: "reapers brave" and "harvest save." Make it clear that John Hyde was indeed a brave reaper.

Chapter 3

Long before the people of India met Praying Hyde, they knew what it was to pray. But their praying was different. Instead of praying to the only true and living God, the people of India prayed to many gods.

When men, women, boys and girls listened to Praying Hyde preach the Gospel and were converted, they had to turn away from the false gods. It was not easy to stop praying to idols, for they had been doing so all their lives.

Show Illustration #9

One of the make-believe gods before which Indians bow is the idol called Ganesh. Ganesh has a man's body, the head of an elephant, and two extra arms and hands. The Indians believe that because it has four hands and arms it can be more helpful to them. And so they bow and pray to their false god, Ganesh.

Ganesh is supposed to like candy and sweet things. It is called "the god of wisdom" and "the god of good luck." When the Indians come to pray to it, they bring sweet things for it to eat. Of course we know it cannot eat them. But if your grandfather, your father, and your mother all told you this was true, you would probably believe it.

John Hyde found the people believing that Ganesh could help them make a journey safely. They said Ganesh could help them to kill a tiger.

Show Illustration #10

The people believed their gods and goddesses liked to ride on the back of a rat. So they said rats were holy and should not be killed. Can you guess what it would be like to live in such a place? The government tried to kill the rats. But many of the people (Hindus) fed and protected the rats. They were afraid Ganesh would be angry if the rats were killed. And they did not want Ganesh to be angry for he might harm them.

Little children take sweets and flowers and bow in prayer before the awful god, Ganesh, because they do not know any better. "We will do our best to please Ganesh," they say.

And there sits Ganesh–an apron covering its elephant trunk. When the children leave, it cannot reach for the sweets and eat them. It cannot smell the flowers. But the children believe it has life and that it can do all these things. They believe this because they have never heard of the one true loving God who wants to give them eternal life.

Praying Hyde prayed many long hours for the boys and girls, men and women of India–often going without food.

Show Illustration #11

John Hyde saw the people of India worshiping another strange idol. This was a goddess called Annpurna. The name *Annpurna* means "goddess of plenty" or "the one who fills with food."

Annpurna stands in a lovely lotus flower. It holds a bowl of rice in one hand and a spoon in the other. The Hindus believe Annpurna can keep them supplied with rice which is what they eat most of the time.

A boy or girl might have a small image of Annpurna in his home. He bows before it, prays to it, and places some of his food in front of it. But Annpurna does not supply him with food, for many starve to death every year.

It was really difficult for Praying Hyde to get these people to turn from their idols and to pray to the God who sent His Son to die on the cross for them.

Show Illustration #12

Even after they accepted the Lord Jesus as their Saviour from sin, it was hard for them to learn how to pray to the God whom they could not see.

Though many truly turned to God from idols, Praying Hyde was concerned for the thousands who still did not know that God loved them and that the Lord Jesus died for them. So John Hyde preached. But mostly he prayed. Then a very wonderful thing happened.

Chapter 4

Do you know what Christians mean when they talk about a revival?

Usually a revival takes place where a large group of people have come together to listen to a preacher. If the speaker is controlled by the Holy Spirit, God uses him to win many to Christ. And during a revival, Christians confess the sins in their lives. The Holy Spirit uses them also to win souls for the Lord Jesus. Whole towns and cities know something has happened when a revival breaks out, because many, many turn to the Lord Jesus for forgiveness of sins and salvation. Do you suppose a preacher can be controlled by the Holy Spirit and used to win souls if he does not spend time with God alone in prayer? Of course not!

One time a famous evangelist was going to Europe to preach. He and his workers held a prayer meeting. Someone who attended the meeting said, "When I opened my eyes and looked around, I saw the evangelist lying flat on his face on the floor. He was praying and begging God to remove all sin from his heart so souls could be saved."

Show Illustration #13

This is the way Praying Hyde often prayed–stretched out on the ground. He prayed so hard and long and went without so many meals that he became seriously ill. But Praying Hyde was willing to give his life in order that souls in India might be saved. And his prayers brought about a wonderful *revival* in that part of India where he preached–and prayed. Many turned to the Lord. It was a wonderful revival for India.

Show Illustration #14

Then Praying Hyde asked God to let him lead one soul to the Lord *every day for a year*. He asked for one soul who would be converted and who would–after his conversion–confess Christ in public before other Hindus.

This meant that Praying Hyde often had to take long journeys to places where God led him. It meant he spent nights in prayer and days without eating. But by the end of that year Praying Hyde had led *over 400* Indian people to the Lord. I think John Hyde would have been happy and satisfied and would stop praying so hard. What do you think?

Instead of being satisfied, Praying Hyde asked God to let him lead *two* souls a day to Christ the next year. At the end of that year 800 more Hindus had placed their trust in the Lord Jesus. Was this because John Hyde was a great preacher? Indeed not! It came about because John Hyde was *Praying* Hyde.

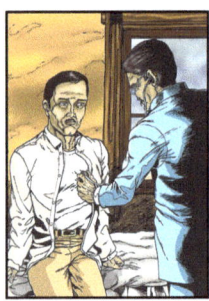

Show Illustration #15

One day John Hyde asked two evangelists to go with him to a distant village. Before leaving, Praying Hyde asked God for ten souls to be saved that day.

They reached the village. They preached and sang. But not one person turned to the Lord. It was late in the day and the evangelists wanted to leave for home to get rest and food. But John Hyde would not go. They stopped at a little cottage and asked a man for water to drink. The man invited them inside and gave them not only water but milk also.

John Hyde spoke to the man and his family about the true and living God and His Son, the Lord Jesus Christ. All nine in the family listened to the Gospel. And every one of them received the Lord Jesus as Saviour that very day! "Now," the two evangelists said, "we must go home. It is getting dark and the road is dangerous."

Show Illustration #16

When the oxcart was ready to take them home, John Hyde did not get in. He was longing for the tenth person for whom he had prayed. The others were getting angry with him.

Just then a nephew of the man who had given them milk arrived in the village. Mr. Hyde went back to the house. And in a short while he led this young man to the Lord! His prayer for the salvation of ten souls was answered.

John Hyde's prayers wore out his body. But he was happy. He did not mind being sick when he saw Hindus being born into the family of God.

Chapter 5

Show Illustration #17

John Hyde prayed so long and so hard that his heart became sick. The doctors said John Hyde would not live. So they sent him home to die. On his way home from India, Praying Hyde stopped in England. There he learned that men from America were holding evangelistic meetings. He went to the meetings.

Praying Hyde could not simply sit and listen in a meeting where sinners needed to be saved. And so John Hyde prayed long and hard for souls to be saved in England.

After Praying Hyde and the evangelists prayed together, many were saved. But this weakened Praying Hyde's body even more.

Show Illustration #18

Finally Praying Hyde got to America and went to stay with a sister. To another he wrote, "Am still in bed or in a wheelchair. Getting a fine rest and doing a lot of the ministry of intercession [praying for others] and having not a few opportunities of personal work [witnessing]."

Soon God called him home to Heaven. John Hyde had given his life in praying for others. Do you suppose he dreaded going to Heaven? How happy he must have been to see the Lord Jesus, face-to-face! How delighted he must have been to be in the presence of the One to whom he had so often prayed!

Show Illustration #19

In the Bible we read of Stephen who was stoned to death for preaching. Stephen was the first Christian martyr. A martyr is a person who dies for something he believes in. Stephen chose to die rather than to stop preaching the Word of God.

We know Stephen pleased God because the Bible tells us that when Stephen looked up to Heaven he saw a wonderful sight: Jesus was waiting for him.

Praying Hyde was a martyr also. He gave his life to preach in the land of India. What caused his death was his pleading with God for the souls of the Hindu people.

Show Illustration #20

I am sure that many Hindus in Heaven will gather around Praying Hyde to say, "Thank you for coming to India to tell us that God loves us and the Lord Jesus died for us. If you had not prayed for us, perhaps we might not have been here."

Will there be souls in Heaven because you have prayed for them? God needs boys and girls, as well as men and women, who will spend time alone with Him in prayer. Will *you* be one?

NOTE TO THE TEACHER

Please note that visualized flash cards for the song "Be A Missionary" are located on page 21-23.

The hymn "Take My Life and Let It Be" may also be used as a fitting conclusion to Praying Hyde's biography. This hymn has been colorfully illustrated in 9" x 12" format and is available from Bible Visuals International.

BE A MISSIONARY

J. IRVIN OVERHOLTZER   WENDELL P. LOVELESS

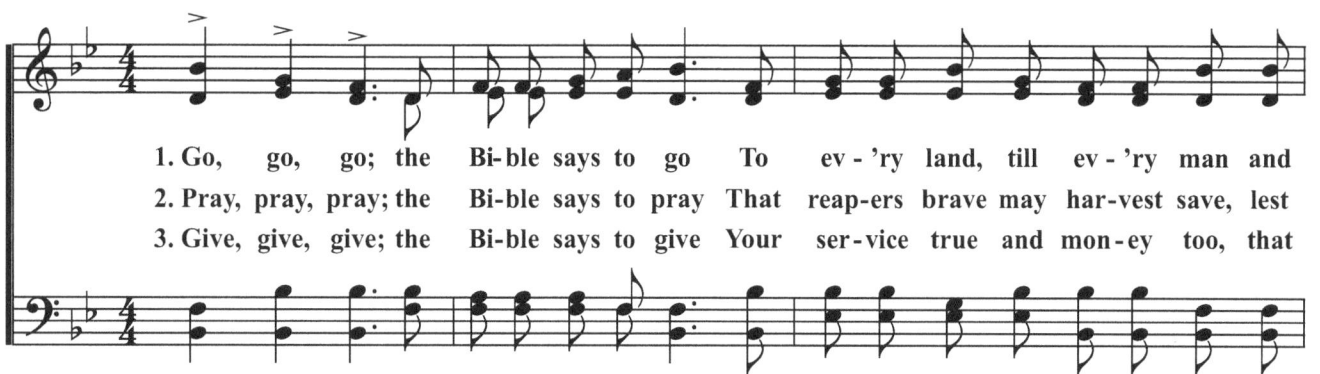

1. Go, go, go; the Bi-ble says to go To ev-'ry land, till ev-'ry man and
2. Pray, pray, pray; the Bi-ble says to pray That reap-ers brave may har-vest save, lest
3. Give, give, give; the Bi-ble says to give Your ser-vice true and mon-ey too, that

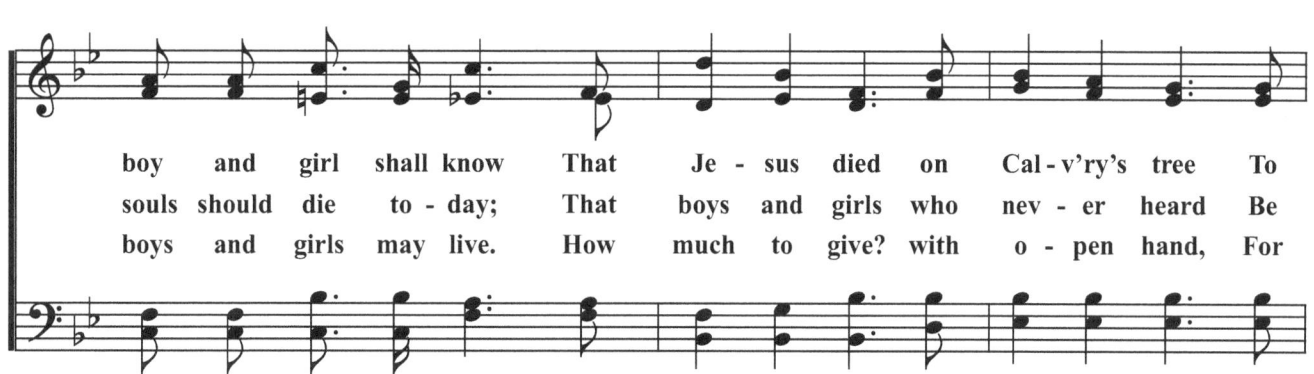

boy and girl shall know That Je-sus died on Cal-v'ry's tree To
souls should die to-day; That boys and girls who nev-er heard Be
boys and girls may live. How much to give? with o-pen hand, For

bring to all sal-va-tion free. Oh, who will go? Oh, will you go?
plain-ly told the bless-ed Word. Oh, who will pray? Oh, will you pray?
Je-sus' sake give all you can. Oh, who will give? Oh, will you give?

Copyright 1938. Renewal 1966 by Ruth P. Overholtzer in Salvation Songs #1
Assigned to Child Evangelism Fellowship, Inc. All rights reserved. Used by permission.
Permission is granted to make one copy of this sheet music for your pianist.

Review Questions
Written by Bryan Willoughby

Chapter 1
1. Who taught John Hyde how to pray? *(His parents)*
2. How old do you think you have to be for your prayers to really matter? *(God listens carefully to everyone's prayers, from the greatest leader to the smallest child.)*
3. Did John have more brothers or sisters? *(Sisters: he had three sisters and two brothers.)*
4. What did John's older brother Edmund go to school to become? *(A missionary)*
5. Why did friends pin Edmond's railroad ticket to his coat? *(They were afraid his high fever might make him crazy, and he could lose the ticket or forget where he was going.)*
6. How long did John pray on the night before he announced that God wanted him to go to a foreign land? *(He stayed up all night praying.)*
7. Besides speaking to God, what did John learn to do while he prayed. *(He learned to listen to God's voice speaking to his heart.)*

Chapter 2
1. What do you think John Hyde thought about during his boat ride to India? *(Perhaps he wondered what plans God had for him in India or thought about his family back in the United States.)*
2. Why did John become so discouraged that he thought about leaving India and going back home? *(He had a difficult time learning the language.)*
3. What two things did John do about his language struggle? *(He prayed to God for help and studied hard.)*
4. How do you think John felt when the people started calling him Praying Hyde? *(He was probably glad. Perhaps it encouraged him to keep on praying.)*
5. What are two things that John gave-up in order to have more time to pray? *(Sleeping and eating)*
6. What did John pray for the most? *(The souls of the people of India)*
7. What do you pray for the most? *(Perhaps thanking God, for guidance, or for the needs of others)*
8. Why do you think John was so sad at the thought of people being forever separated from God? *(Perhaps because he knew what a wonderful thing it was to be very close to God and how terrible it would be to not have that relationship.)*
9. How did the people John prayed for learn about Jesus? *(From hearing John or someone else preach)*
10. Why was it hard for the people of India to leave their religion? *(It was the only religion they had ever known.)*

Chapter 3
1. How were John's prayers different from the prayers of those who followed the Indian religion? *(John prayed to the Living God while others prayed to idols that could not even hear them.)*
2. What Indian idol has a human body with the head of an elephant? *(Ganesh)*
3. What does Ganesh have that is supposed to make it more helpful? *(Two extra arms and hands)*
4. What do you think eventually happens to the uneaten sweets that are placed before Ganesh? *(Perhaps the rats and insects nibble on them or they are thrown in the trash after a day or two.)*
5. Why do the people believe that rats are holy? *(They believe that gods and goddesses ride on their backs.)*
6. What did many Hindu people do when the government tried to kill the rats? *(They fed and protected them.)*
7. What idol's name means "goddess of plenty?" *(Annpurna)*
8. What does Annpurna hold in her hands? *(A bowl of rice and a spoon)*
9. Why was it hard for new Indian Christians to pray to God? *(They couldn't see Him like they could see an idol.)*
10. What might you say to encourage someone who is having trouble praying to God? *(Suggest they close their eyes when they pray; tell them it will become easier with practice.)*

Chapter 4
1. What is a revival? *(Many people in a town/city turn to God for forgiveness of sins and decide to live for Him.)*
2. What is a soul? *(This is the part of each person that stays alive after his or her body dies.)*
3. In what position did Praying Hyde often pray? *(Stretched out on the ground)*
4. Praying Hyde asked God for one new Christian every day for a year. What else did he want each of these people to do? *(Publicly share Jesus with other Hindus)*
5. Did Praying Hyde reach his goal of one new Christian every day? *(Yes, over 400 people became Christians in that one year.)*
6. Who did John Hyde ask to travel with him to a distant village? *(Two evangelists)*
7. Why did these two evangelists become angry with Praying Hyde? *(Because he did not want to return home, even though nine people had come to know Jesus and it was getting dark and dangerous to travel.)*
8. Who was the tenth person to become a Christian that day? *(The nephew of the man who had given them milk)*
9. What was John's attitude like when he became sick? *(He did not let his sickness bother him, but was happy because Hindus were becoming part of God's family.)*
10. Can you think of any other nicknames that might be good for Praying Hyde? *(Perhaps Caring Hyde, Ambitious Hyde or Persistent Hyde)*

Chapter 5
1. What part of Praying Hyde's body was making him sick? *(His heart)*
2. What country did John Hyde stop in on his way back to the United States? *(England)*
3. Why do you think praying weakened John's body? *(Often he would go without the food and rest that his body needed, and his deep concern for those who did not know Jesus put him under great stress.)*
4. What did John do with his time when he returned to the United States? *(Rested, prayed, and shared with others about Jesus)*
5. Do you think it was easier or harder for John to pray when he was confined to a wheelchair and his bed? *(Perhaps easier because he had more time and less distractions and responsibilities.)*
6. Praying Hyde's greatest desire in life was to see others come to know Jesus. How might his attitude have been different if he was living for himself? *(He might have been angry about becoming sick and having to leave India.)*
7. Why was Stephen stoned to death? *(For preaching the Word of God)*
8. What advice do you think Praying Hyde might give to Christians if he were alive today? *(He would probably encourage them to pray more.)*
9. What are some things you can do to have a better prayer life? *(Set aside some time every day for prayer, keep a prayer journal, ask a friend to remind you to pray.)*

www.ingramcontent.com/pod-product-compliance
Lightning Source LLC
Chambersburg PA
CBHW060800090426
42736CB00002B/103